Florentine Embroidery

*The complete guide to working Florentine stitches
from choosing the right canvas to blocking the finished
embroidery with over 50 patterns to embroider*

Florentine Embroidery

All you need to know for perfect results

by

Barbara Müller

THORSONS PUBLISHING GROUP

First UK Edition published 1989

First published in Germany by
Rosenheimer Verlagshaus,
Am Stocket 12, D-8200 Rosenheim 2, Germany

© Patterns and charts Barbara Müller 1986
© English text Thorsons Publishing Group 1989

British Library Cataloguing in Publication Data

Müller, Barbara
Florentine embroidery: the complete guide
to working Florentine stitches from
choosing the right canvas to blocking the
finished embroidery with over 50 patterns
to embroider.
1. Italian embroidery
I. Title
746.44'0945

ISBN 0-7225-1815-3

*Published by Thorsons Publishers Limited,
Wellingborough, Northamptonshire NN8 2RQ, England*

Translated by Janet Winslow
Craft Editor, Eileen Lowcock
Embroideries and patterns prepared by Barbara Müller
Photographs on page 14 by Fritz Höllerer, remaining photographs
including cover, by Foto-Rammel
Typeset by Harper Phototypesetters Limited, Northampton, England
Printed in Italy by G. Canale & C. S.p.A., Turin

1 3 5 7 9 10 8 6 4 2

Contents

Introduction

Florentine embroidery is a type of canvas work or embroidery on canvas, erroneously called tapestry, tapestry being a woven textile. In America, canvas embroidery is referred to as needlepoint. In England, needlepoint can also refer to a type of needle-made lace.

Florentine embroidery is known by various names: in America it is called Bargello and in Italy, they refer to it as 'punto fiamma' (flame stitch). Sometimes it is also called Water stitch or Hungarian stitch.

The best way to describe Florentine embroidery is to say it is a stepped satin stitch and endless pattern variations can be created by varying the length and step of the stitch, and the colours. The interaction of colours is essential, whether they are subtle or brash. Whether they are graduated shades of different colours or simply shades of one colour, the charm of Florentine embroidery lies entirely in the colours.

The technique is an old one. You can find very early examples dating from the thirteenth century. However, this type of embroidery really only became fashionable in the seventeenth century. Unfortunately, its precise origin has not been researched. It is said that a Hungarian princess once married a young man from the Medici family in Florence. Her bridal outfit was decorated in a most beautiful fashion with embroidery in Hungarian stitch. She then went on to teach the art of this stitch to the enthusiastic ladies at the Florentine Court.

Another story will have us believe that prisoners serving their sentences in the Bargello Palace were kept occupied with embroidery. If you know this palace, which today houses the National Museum, you will certainly not believe this story.

Wherever this type of embroidery may have originated, it quickly found many supporters throughout Europe and through the English *émigrés* it even reached America. There it developed in a highly individual way where very bright colour combinations were used.

Today, the art of Florentine embroidery is enjoying renewed popularity due to the speed and ease with which it can be worked and the way in which the designs fit in with modern styles.

I hope you will get much pleasure from Florentine embroidery and I wish you every success in your endeavours.

Materials

Canvas

Florentine embroidery is generally worked on canvas, which is a coarse, evenly woven fabric, usually made of cotton and stiffened with sizing to retain its shape. Linen canvas, which is extra hard-wearing, is also available but it is expensive. Canvas can be purchased by the metre (yard) and is made in widths ranging from 45cm (18 in) to 150cm (60 in). It is produced in various mesh sizes that are determined by the number of holes per 2.5cm (1 in), and can be obtained in either white or ecru. If you are planning a piece of work with predominantly light colours, choose white canvas but choose ecru if you are using dark colours. This will avoid the canvas showing through the stitching.

Mono or single-weave canvas, which has evenly spaced warp and weft threads is ideal for Florentine embroidery. Mono canvas comes in mesh sizes varying from 14 to 26 holes per 2.5cm (1 in). To begin with try a 16 or 18 mesh canvas.

Penelope canvas has double threads for each mesh. With this type of weave however, the threads are unequally spaced and have to be split when working Florentine embroidery. It is therefore difficult to cover it evenly with stitches and the thread frays easily.

Rug canvas is available in both mono and Penelope canvas — a mesh size of 10 to 12 in mono canvas being suitable for Florentine rugs. It is available in widths of 90, 100 and 135cm (36, 40 and 54 in).

Even-weave fabrics

For fine work, even-weave fabrics such as cotton and linen, especially produced for embroidery purposes, can be used in conjunction with stranded cotton, pearl cotton or soft embroidery cotton threads. Dress or upholstery fabrics cannot be relied upon to be of accurate even-weave. If the correct fabric is not used, the shape of the designs will be distorted.

Threads

For Florentine embroidery on canvas, it is advisable to use woollen threads specially made for embroidery. These are hard wearing and available in a vast range of colours whereas knitting yarns are softer and have a tendency to wear thin while being worked and pile easily in wear.

It is important in Florentine embroidery, that the stitches completely cover the background material otherwise the embroidery looks unattractive and will show signs of wear quickly.

Unless the work is for purely decorative purposes, such as a wall-hanging, it is unwise to mix yarn types in one project.

The woollen yarns available for Florentine embroidery are: Tapestry wool, useful on 16 to 18 mesh canvas; Crewel wool, a hard-wearing stranded yarn that can be used from two strands upwards in the needle on most mesh sizes; Persian yarns, which are of a high quality, are hard-wearing and available in an outstanding colour range, are also stranded; carpet thrums (available from carpet manufacturers), are supplied in bags of mixed co-ordinating colours and are inexpensive and hard-wearing.

Preparing the canvas

Before you begin to embroider, outline the pattern pieces on the canvas using a pencil or tacking stitches.

If you want to make a chair-seat cover it is advisable to have the pattern prepared for you by an experienced upholsterer who will cover the seat for you when the embroidery has been completed. Don't forget to allow for the stitchery shrinking the canvas slightly and to add a border of at least 5cm (2 in) on all edges for seam allowance and blocking.

Once the design is marked on the canvas, enclose the raw edges in folded masking tape, or fold and tack wide cotton tape over them to prevent the canvas from unravelling and catching the embroidery yarns while working.

Colours

Once you have decided what you are going to embroider, consider what the finished design will be used for and, if it is to be used as a household item, where it is to be placed. Take great care in choosing the colours as these are the essence of Florentine embroidery. With chair covers or cushions for example, the colours should complement the other furnishings in the room. Select colours from curtains or a rug for example, and use shades of these in the embroidery.

The colour suggestions given with the individual patterns are not hard and fast rules, merely guide-lines for those who are not practised in working with colours.

If you lack confidence in choosing colours, select shades of one colour or subtle colours rather than brightly coloured ones. The total graduations of a colour as used in the pattern on page 48, can be extremely attractive.

Embroidery frame

Since Florentine stitches are not so likely to distort the canvas as some stitches when worked, it is not necessary to work small pieces in a frame. It is easier however, to handle larger items in a rectangular frame (or the work may be stapled onto an old picture frame), which holds the canvas taught so that the stitches lie in an even tension on top of the work. As the stitches are worked in a stabbing movement, the use of a frame has the additional advantage of leaving both hands free to work the stitches. The right hand remains on top of the frame, inserting the needle, and the left hand remains beneath the frame, to receive and return the needle to the right side of the work for the next stitch. A tambour or round frame is not suitable for use with canvas as it distorts the shape of the canvas.

Needles

Those with a long eye and a rounded point, sold as tapestry or rug needles, are available in a variety of numbered sizes. The smaller the number, the coarser the needle. Numbers 18 and 20 are the most useful to have. Number 14 is ideal for use with thicker yarns and number 26 should be used for finer yarns, such as stranded cotton. Packets of mixed needles can be obtained but these contain mainly fine needles, so it is better to obtain one-size packets of the most useful sizes. The eye of the needle should be large enough to take the yarn freely and the needle itself of a size large enough to draw the yarn smoothly through the canvas without strain.

Thimble

To protect the finger from the continuous pressure and friction of the needle and to ensure that the needle is being held in a correct manner, a well-fitting thimble is essential.

Scissors

Two pairs of sharp scissors will be needed: one for cutting the canvas and a small, pointed pair for cutting the yarn.

Blocking

Canvas work embroidery should never be pressed with an iron as this flattens the texture of the stitches and can completely ruin a piece of work. Most pieces, however, do benefit from being blocked.

Cover a flat surface such as a drawing board or an old unpolished table with a clean towel, or several sheets of white blotting paper. Place the work right side down on this padding and thoroughly dampen it by dabbing with a sponge and clean water, but be careful not to soak the work. This initial dampening makes the canvas more flexible and easier to handle during the following stages.

Using the straight edge of the board as a guide, commence at the centre on one long side and pin securely with rustless drawing pins, gently but firmly pulling and pinning from the centre outwards, left and right alternately, at 2.5cm (1 in) intervals. Continue in the same way along the next side until the whole piece of work is pinned firmly into shape. If the work has dried out slightly during this process, dampen it again evenly all over. Cover the work with another clean towel or several sheets of blotting paper and weight it evenly with books or some other heavy, flat object. Leave to dry for at least 48 hours.

When the work is completely dry, remove the pins and trim the excess canvas to the required seam allowance (not less than 1.5cm (⅝ in) on fine canvas and not less than 2.5cm (1 in) on coarse canvas). Oversew all edges to prevent fraying before making up. If the work is being used for upholstery purposes, do not trim the excess canvas off at this stage.

Uses of Florentine embroidery

Classically, Florentine embroidery was used in making covers for chair and stool tops, armchairs, bed covers and even whole wallcoverings were embroidered in this way.

Today, few people have the time to embroider such large projects. However, many an old footstool or chair seat can be restored to its former glory with Florentine work and elegant upholstery.

When a large-mesh canvas and thick wool are chosen, the end result could be an original rug which can be used to highlight an area in the home. If, however, a finer mesh is chosen, the embroidery will be suitable for smaller items such as curtain ties or belts.

Florentine embroidery looks particularly elegant when it is worked very finely with stranded cotton on an even-weave fabric. Clothes can be embellished in this way, for example, imagine the wave pattern shown on page 43 on the yoke and narrow straps of a summer dress.

Pockets, purses, cushions, photograph albums, chest covers, table runners and small bed covers are all perfect subjects for decoration, depending on your enthusiasm and the time available. Wherever a surface pattern is needed, Florentine embroidery is particularly suitable. It is not however, suitable for borders, on tablecloths for example. It works best as an all-over embroidery to fill flat surfaces.

Choosing the design

When choosing a design you must consider the size of the pattern repeat in relation to the area to be embroidered. For example, if you can only see the pattern repeat twice on a footstool pad, the charm of Florentine embroidery will not be fully appreciated. You should therefore be able to see several pattern repeats both horizontally and vertically.

When making your selection, look at the pattern from a distance. If you place the book a little distance away from you, you will notice that some patterns have a fluid look. This is an important point to consider when choosing a pattern.

All the wave and jagged patterns can be altered quite easily. You only need to vary the length of the stitch, working over 4 or 6 threads of canvas. Note, however,

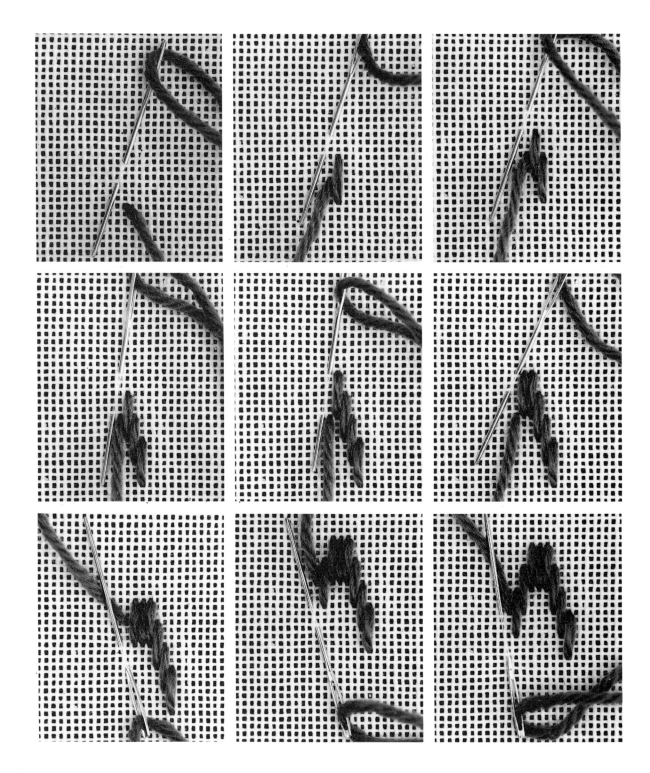

that a pattern which is shown in the book worked over 4 threads will look steeper when it is stitched over 6 threads. A pattern worked over 6 threads on the other hand will look flatter when worked over 4 threads. Once you are familiar with the technique you will realize the countless possibilities.

Commencing work

You generally work Florentine embroidery from right to left. This means you should start at the bottom right-hand corner of the work following the Florentine stitch pattern. It is particularly important to count this row carefully as any mistakes made here are repeated throughout the whole piece of work. The pattern repeats are marked on the charts with an X at the beginning and end.

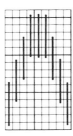

Avoid making knots in the embroidery yarn as they tend to unravel. Begin work by leaving a length of yarn on the right side of the work, taking it to the back and working it in later. Work all other thread ends into the back of the work as you go.

The way to stitch is shown in the photographs opposite, bearing in mind that the steps are shown scooping the canvas whereas, in reality, the stitches are worked in a stabbing motion. Continue working row after row as shown. At the top and lower edges, the stitches should be shortened accordingly to half stitch length in order to make a straight edging.

With trellis patterns do not begin at the edge but start further into the canvas. First embroider a large section of the borders, then fill in. Threads that are not needed at any time should be brought to the front of the work and left hanging until they are needed again.

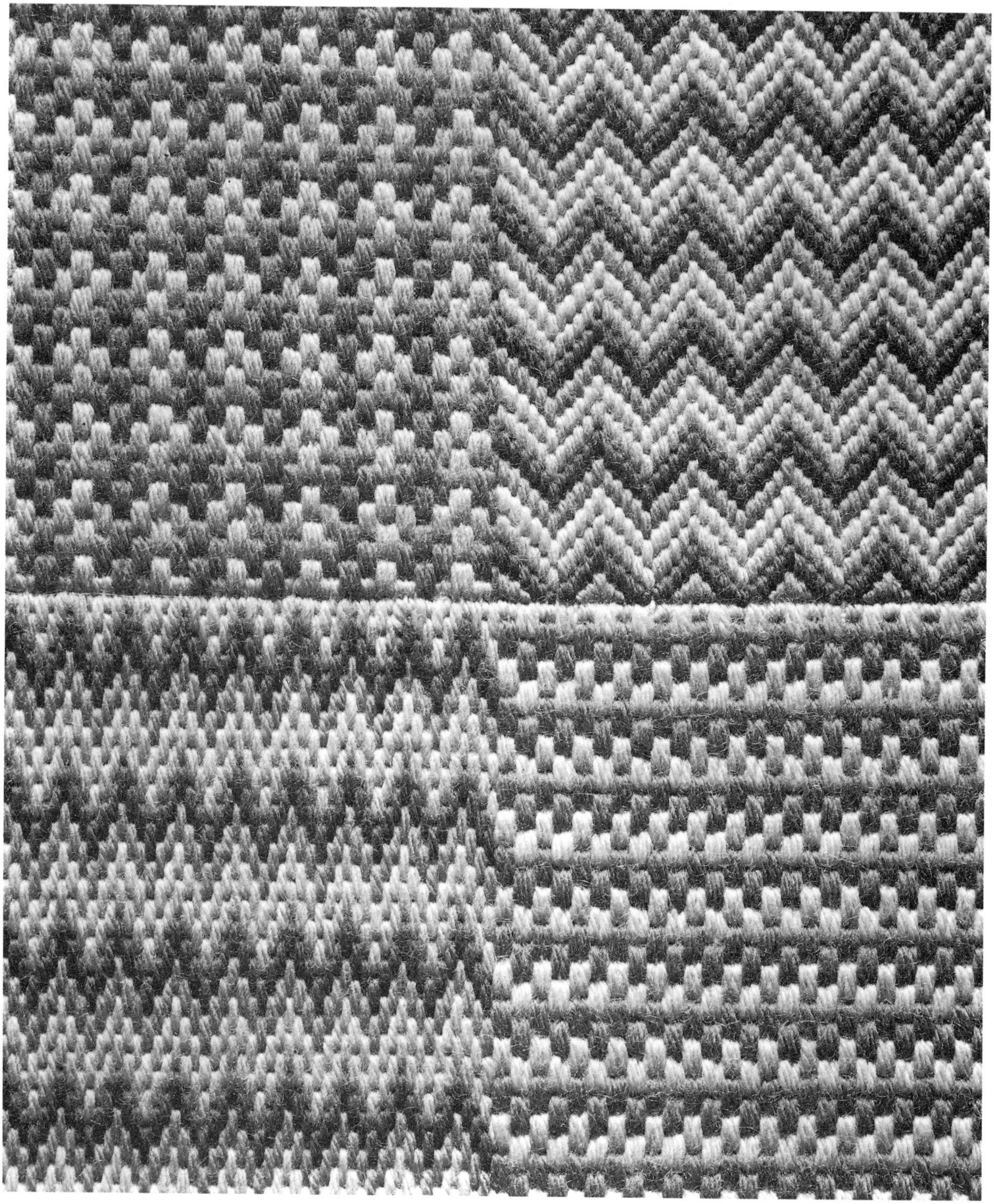

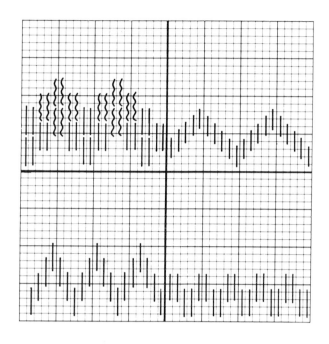

Four small patterns for practise or for small
objects.

<table>
<tr><td>Top left:</td><td></td><td>Top right:</td><td></td></tr>
<tr><td>Light sea-green</td><td>Nr. 3140</td><td>Light sea-green</td><td>Nr. 3140</td></tr>
<tr><td>Dark sea-green</td><td>Nr. 3050</td><td>Light brown</td><td>Nr. 3134</td></tr>
<tr><td></td><td></td><td>Mid brown</td><td>Nr. 3065</td></tr>
<tr><td>Bottom left:</td><td></td><td>Dark brown</td><td>Nr. 3136</td></tr>
<tr><td>Light sea-green</td><td>Nr. 3140</td><td></td><td></td></tr>
<tr><td>Light brown</td><td>Nr. 3134</td><td>Bottom right:</td><td></td></tr>
<tr><td>Mid brown</td><td>Nr. 3065</td><td>Light sea-green</td><td>Nr. 3139</td></tr>
<tr><td>Dark brown</td><td>Nr. 3136</td><td>Dark sea-green</td><td>Nr. 3050</td></tr>
</table>

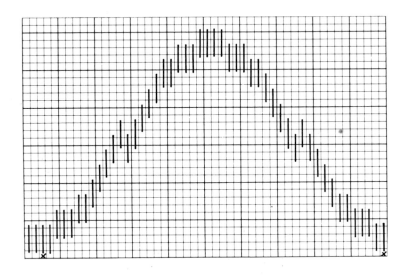

A classical pattern that should be
embroidered particularly neatly. It is worked
here over 4 threads of canvas.

Lightest green	Nr. 3085
Light green	Nr. 3087
Mid green	Nr. 3043
Dark green	Nr. 3089
White	Nr. 3204
Lightest brown	Nr. 3134
Light brown	Nr. 3065
Mid brown	Nr. 3136
Dark brown	Nr. 3040
Pink	Nr. 3893
Dark pink	Nr. 3895
Red	Nr. 3896
Dark red	Nr. 3898

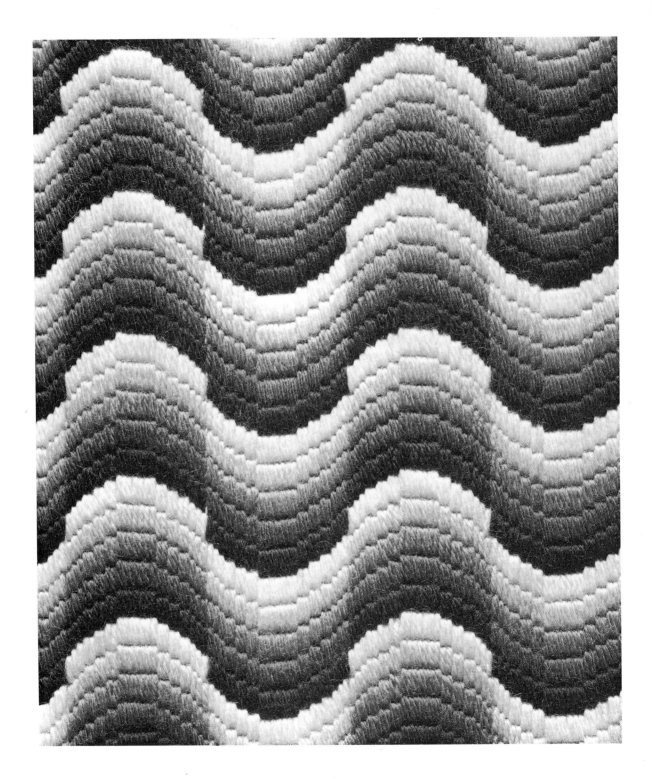

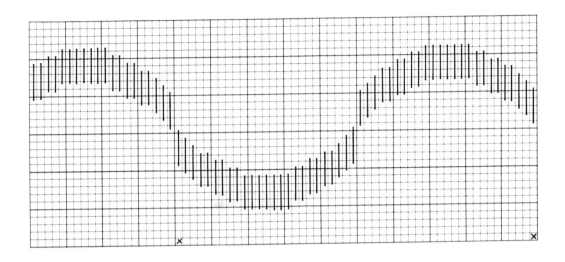

This pattern has a fluid look when seen from a distance. It
is therefore particularly suitable for larger objects.

Dark red	Nr. 3898
Mid red	Nr. 3896
Light red	Nr. 3895
Lightest red	Nr. 3893
White	Nr. 3222

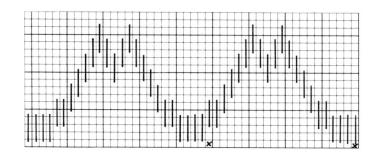

Different stitch lengths were used in this
pattern.

Red	Nr. 3009	over 4 threads
Light blue	Nr. 3445	over 4 threads
Green	Nr. 3177	over 5 threads
Yellow	Nr. 3085	over 4 threads
Brown	Nr. 3137	over 3 threads

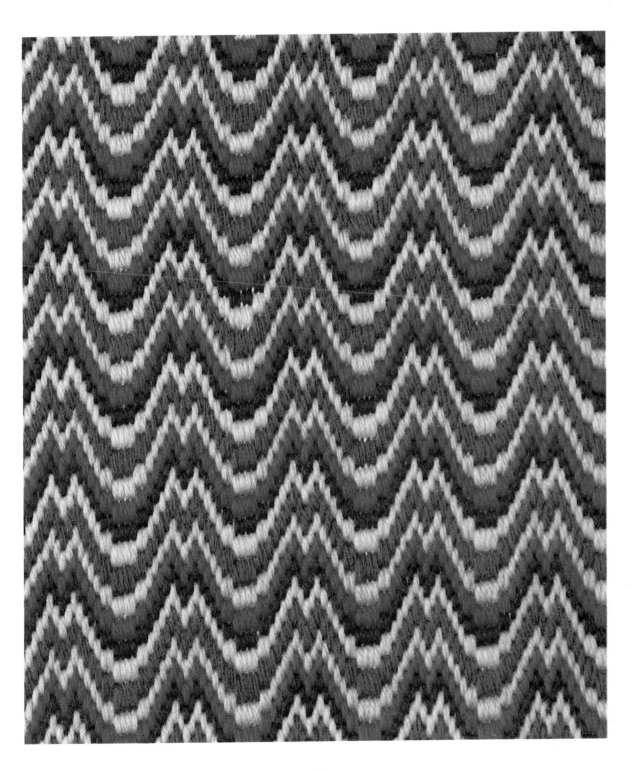

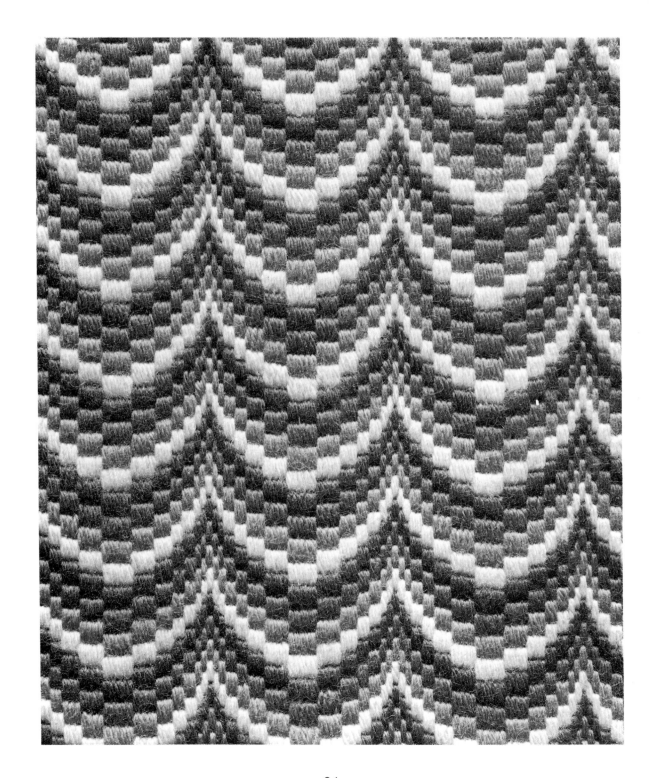

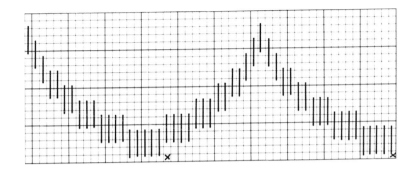

This is a very simple pattern that can easily
be adapted. If you are embroidering large
surfaces you can embroider over 6 threads of
canvas. You can also reverse it so that the
curves go up. There are countless colour
possibilities. In this case four tones of blue
were used.

Light blue	Nr. 3144
Mid blue	Nr. 3146
Darker blue	Nr. 3058
Dark blue	Nr. 3034

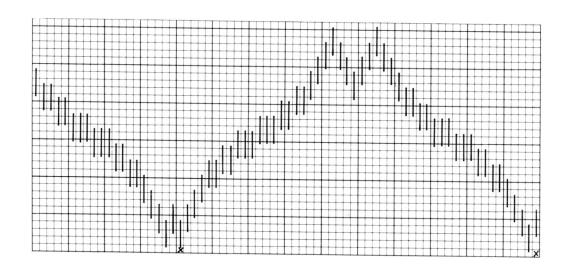

White	Nr. 3204
Turquoise	Nr. 3140
White	Nr. 3204
Pale violet	Nr. 3155
Mid violet	Nr. 3157
Dark violet	Nr. 3158
Mid violet	Nr. 3157
Pale violet	Nr. 3155

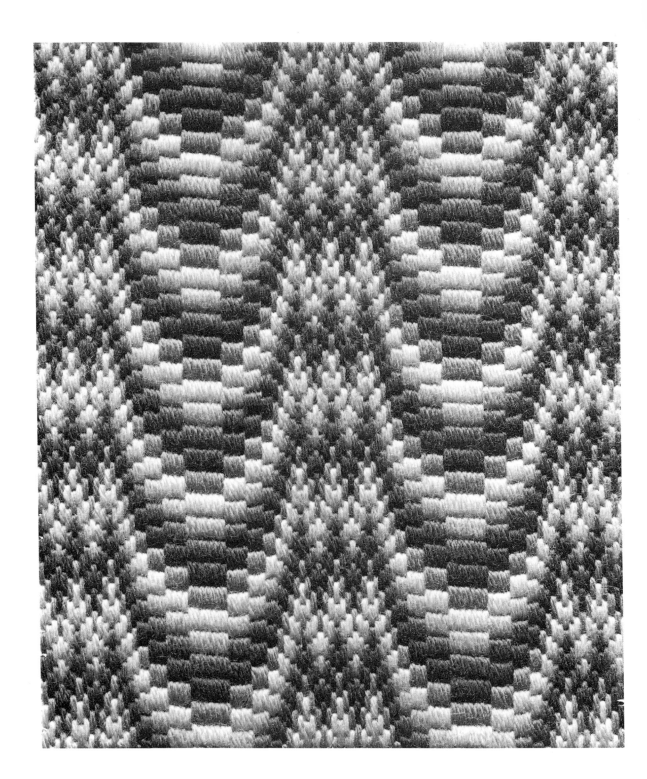

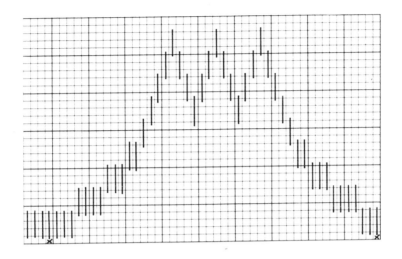

This pattern is embroidered over 4 threads of canvas, then stepped up or down by 3 threads. It is, therefore, a rather jagged pattern and is only suitable for larger surfaces such as chair coverings. You could also step it by 2 threads and then the curves become flatter and more gentle.

Light green	Nr. 3175
Dark green	Nr. 3180
Dark yellow	Nr. 3015
Mid yellow	Nr. 3013
Pale yellow	Nr. 3229

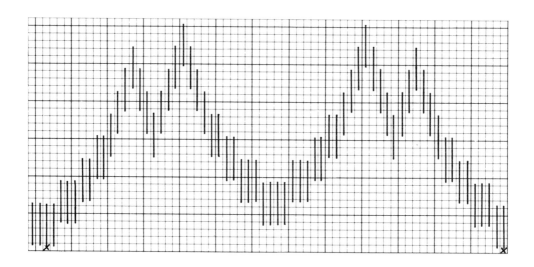

Embroider this over 6 threads of canvas and then step up or down by 3 threads. You could also embroider it over 4 threads (stepping by 2 threads) but you would not achieve such a striking effect.

Darkest green	Nr. 3078
Red	Nr. 3011
Darkest green	Nr. 3078
Lighter green	Nr. 3050
Grey	Nr. 3094
Lighter green (twice)	Nr. 3050

This pattern was also used for the embroidery shown on the cover but there it was worked in stranded cotton. On a background of even-weave linen with 30 threads per 2.5cm (1 in). 3 strands of stranded cotton were used in the following colours:

Darkest green	Nr. 217
Lighter green	Nr. 215
Lightest green (instead of grey)	Nr. 213
Lighter green (twice)	Nr. 896
Darkest green	
Dark pink	

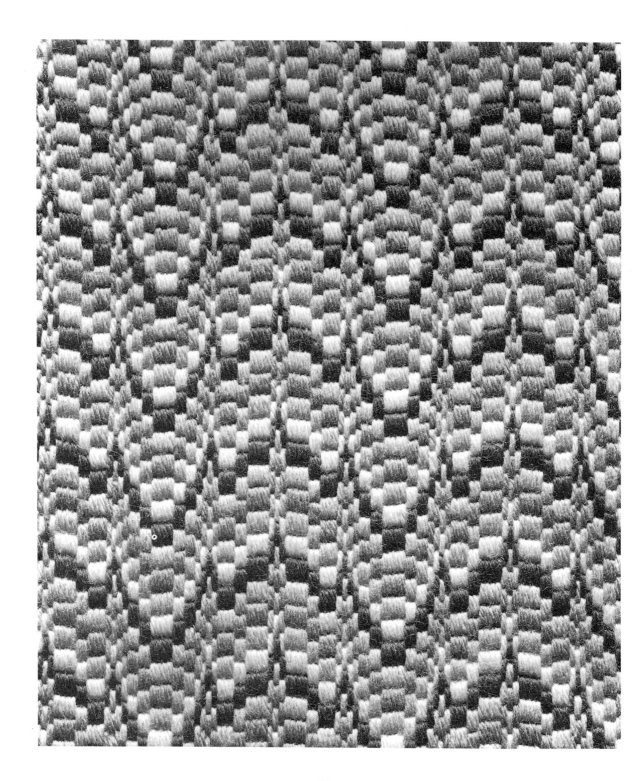

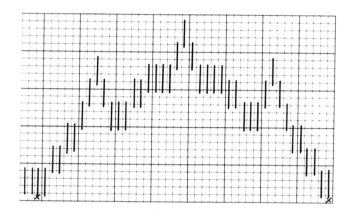

This pattern is embroidered over 4
threads of canvas and can be stepped up
or down by 3 threads. Only in one
place, near the centre, is it set around 2
threads.

Pale yellow	Nr. 3229
Mid yellow	Nr. 3013
Green	Nr. 3175
Blue	Nr. 3094
Brown	Nr. 3016

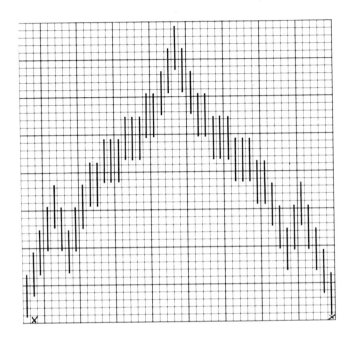

You could also use this pattern in
reverse.

Red	Nr. 3011
Pale yellow	Nr. 3229
Dark yellow	Nr. 3013
Green	Nr. 3044
Dark yellow	Nr. 3013
Pale yellow	Nr. 3229

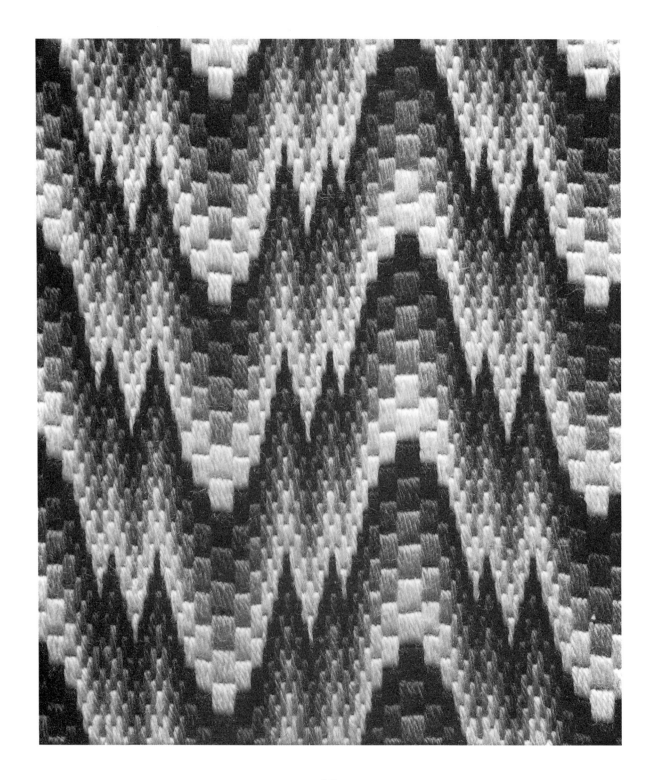

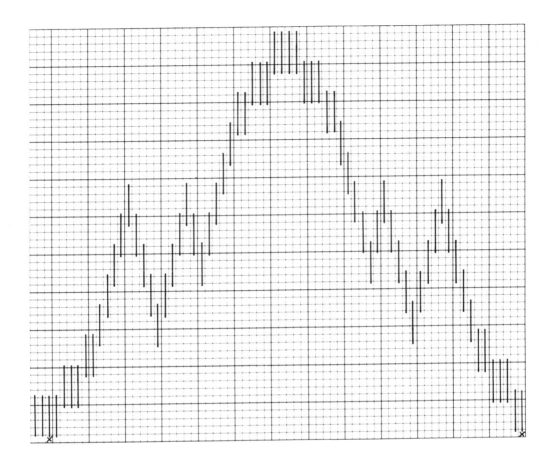

The repeat on this pattern is so large that it is
only suitable for projects with large surfaces.
It is embroidered over 6 threads of canvas
and at times stepped up or down by 4
threads.

Pale pink	Nr. 3290
Pink	Nr. 3893
Light red	Nr. 3895
Red	Nr. 3896
Dark red	Nr. 3898
Black	Nr. 3056

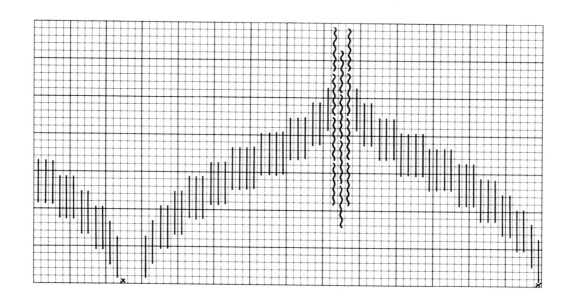

Embroider over 6 threads of canvas and step up or
down by 4 threads. In this pattern the colours are
arranged alternately so that the pattern creates an
optical illusion.

Light brown	Nr. 3134
Mid brown	Nr. 3065
Dark brown	Nr. 3040
White	Nr. 3204
Light green	Nr. 3173
Dark green	Nr. 3180
Blue	Nr. 3030 (for the dividing strips)

For smaller surfaces you can also embroider this
pattern over 4 threads of canvas, stepped up or
down by 2 threads.

Light blue	Nr. 3445
Mid blue	Nr. 3077
Pink	Nr. 3895
Mid blue	Nr. 3077
Light blue	Nr. 3445
Mid blue	Nr. 3077
Dark red	Nr. 3898

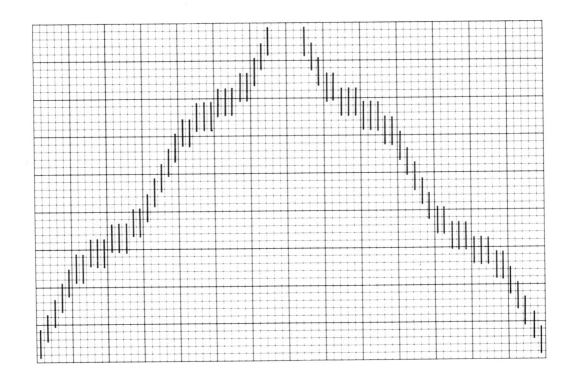

The pattern shown opposite was embroidered from bottom right to top left as shown in the diagram on the right, above. If you are left-handed or you wish to have the slope in the other direction, work according to the drawing on the left.

Dark green	Nr. 3177
Mid green	Nr. 3175
Light green (twice)	Nr. 3173
Mid Green	Nr. 3175
Dark green	Nr. 3177
Pink	Nr. 3290
Dark pink	Nr. 3895
Red	Nr. 3896
Dark red (twice)	Nr. 3898
Red	Nr. 3896
Dark pink	Nr. 3895
Pink	Nr. 3290

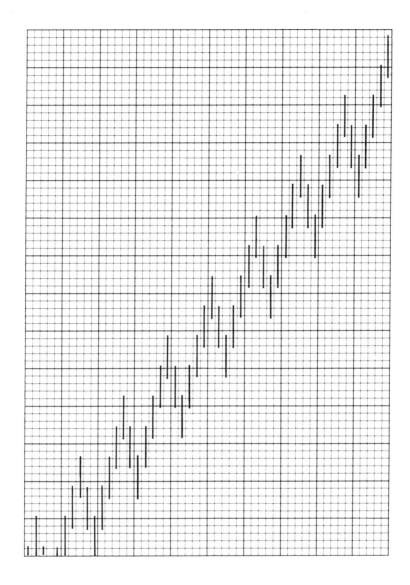

With this sharp, jagged pattern it is best to start work in the top right-hand corner. Count carefully when working the bottom edge as the top of some sharp points still appear. If you don't embroider these points the pattern will not be successful.

Lightest green (twice)	Nr. 3085	Pink	Nr. 3098
Mid green	Nr. 3087	Darkest green	Nr. 3089
Dark green	Nr. 3043	Dark green	Nr. 3043
Darkest green	Nr. 3089	Mid green	Nr. 3087

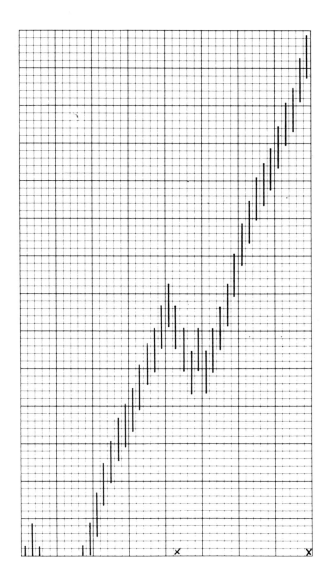

Work from top right to bottom left. At the bottom edge, continue the points as shown in the diagram. Pay careful attention to the variable positions of the individual stitches.

Dark red	Nr. 3011
Mid red	Nr. 3009
Light red	Nr. 3098
Fawn (three times)	Nr. 3139

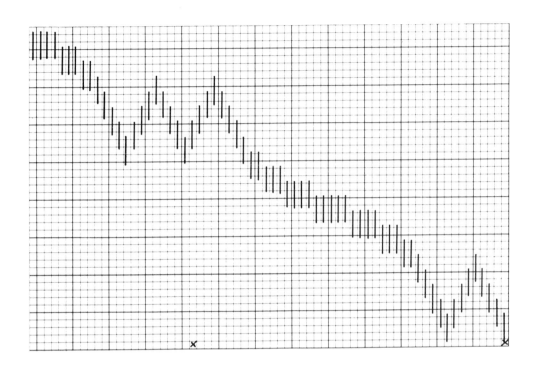

Darkest brown	Nr. 3040
Dark brown	Nr. 3136
Mid brown	Nr. 3065
Light brown	Nr. 3134
White	Nr. 3204

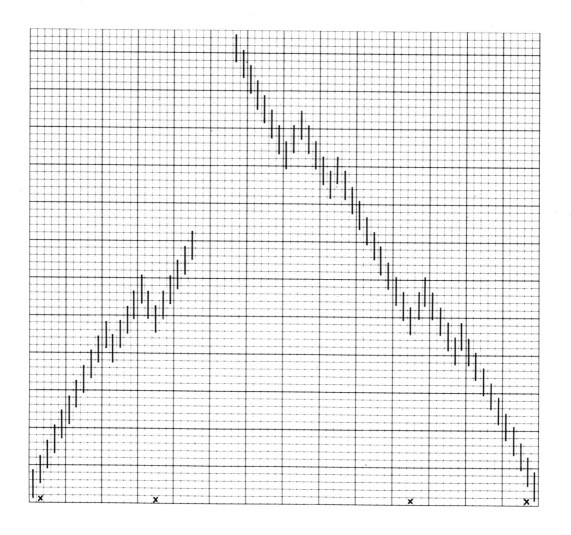

This pattern is embroidered from bottom right to top left as shown in the right-hand diagram above. If you are left-handed or want the pattern to flow in the opposite direction, use the left-hand drawing and work from bottom left to top right.

Red	Nr. 3011	Dark sea-green	Nr. 3078
White	Nr. 3204	Mid sea-green	Nr. 3050
Lightest sea-green	Nr. 3139	Light sea-green	Nr. 3140
Light sea-green	Nr. 3140	Lightest sea-green	Nr. 3139
Mid sea-green	Nr. 3050	White	Nr. 3204

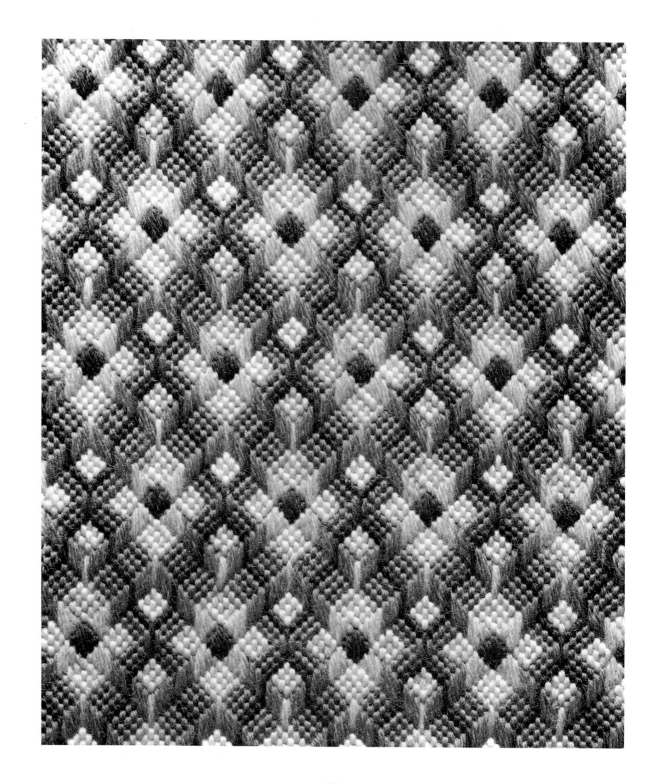

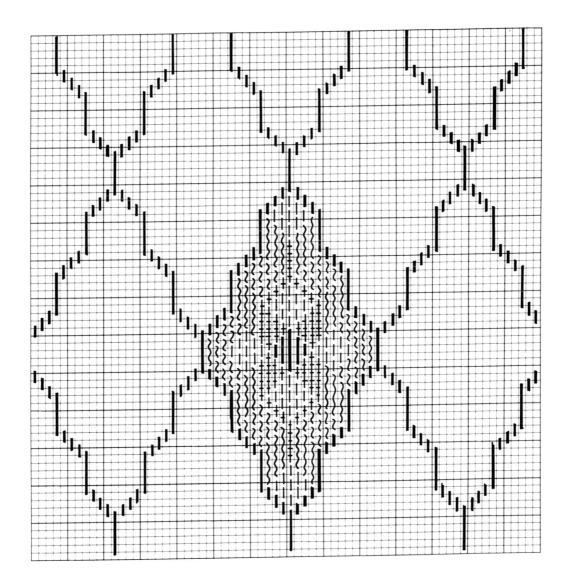

Embroider the dark blue borders first, then
fill in each rhombus in turn.

| = Nr. 3034   Dark blue
} = Nr. 3146   Mid blue
⁞ = Nr. 3144   Pale blue
| = Nr. 3222   White

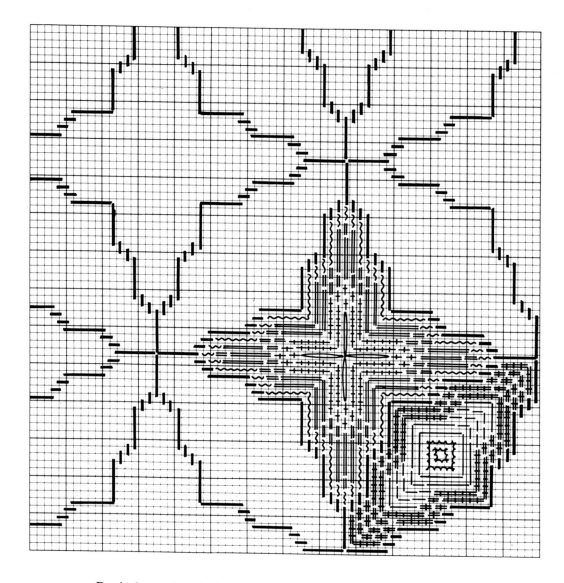

Begin by embroidering a fairly large section of the dark green borders. You will soon notice if you have made a mistake in counting. It is not so easy to make mistakes inside the shapes.

| = Nr. 3180   Dark green

| = Nr. 3175   Mid green

| = Nr. 3173   Light green

| = Nr. 3204   White

| = Nr. 3155   Pale lilac

‖ = Nr. 3157   Mid lilac

: = Nr. 3158   Dark lilac

: = Nr. 3056   Black

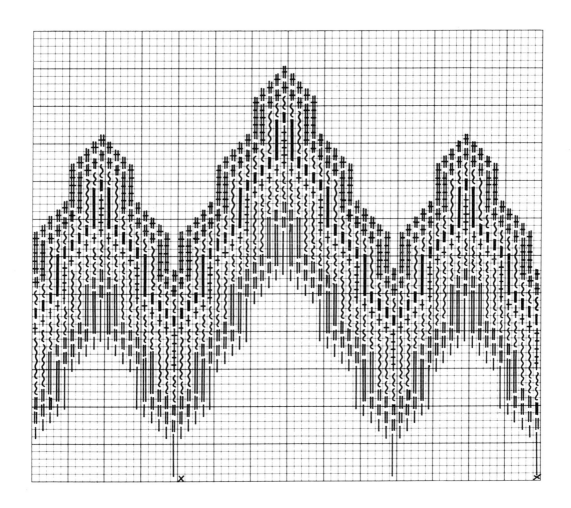

| = Nr. 3222   White
‖ = Nr. 3094   Light blue
≶ = Nr. 3077   Mid blue
⋮ = Nr. 3173   Light green
| = Nr. 3175   Green
⋮ = Nr. 3030   Dark blue

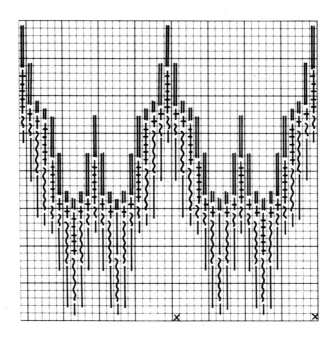

The four different rows of stitches
are always repeated in the same
sequence.

Red	Nr. 3098
Light blue	Nr. 3146
Mid blue	Nr. 3058
Dark blue	Nr. 3034
Light green	Nr. 3173
Mid green	Nr. 3175
Dark green	Nr. 3177
Mid green	Nr. 3175
Light green	Nr. 3173
Dark blue	Nr. 3034
Mid blue	Nr. 3058
Light blue	Nr. 3146

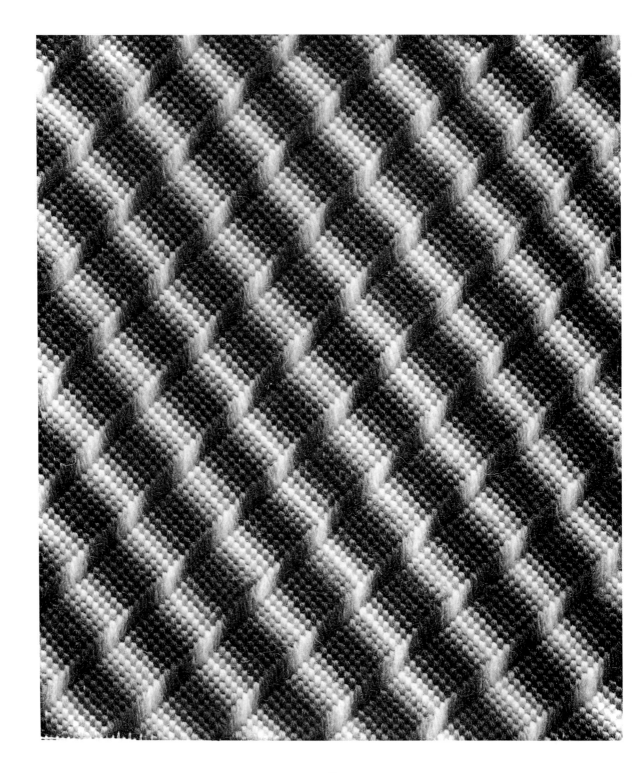

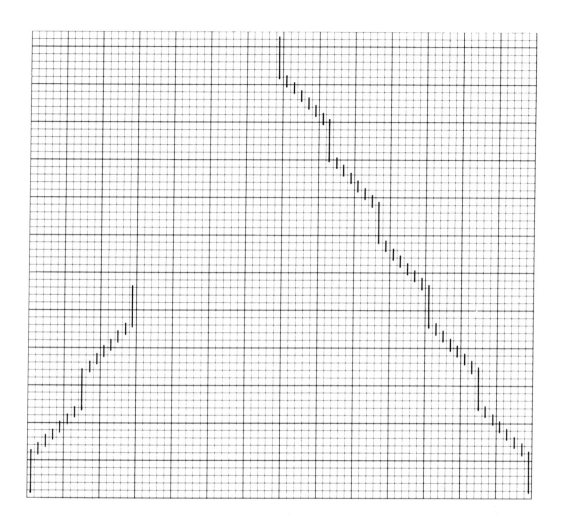

You should embroider this pattern from bottom right to top left. (Left-handers should use the left-hand drawing and work from bottom left to top right.)

White	Nr. 3204	Darkest green	Nr. 3089
Lightest green	Nr. 3085	Dark brown	Nr. 3137
Light green	Nr. 3087	Mid brown	Nr. 3136
Mid green	Nr. 3043	Light brown	Nr. 3065
Dark green	Nr. 3044	Lightest brown	Nr. 3134

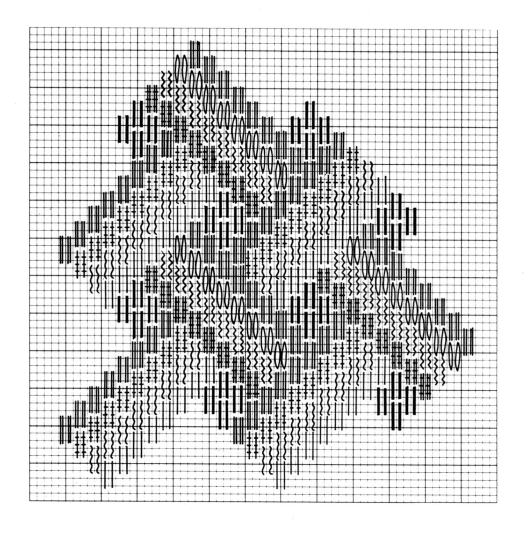

To simplify this pattern you should start working all the colours in turn at the same time. If you do not need a particular thread at any time, let it hand in front of the last stitch on the right side of the work. In this way they will not become tangled at the back.

	= Nr. 3078	Dark green		= Nr. 3030	Dark blue
‖ = Nr. 3445	Pale grey	⁞ = Nr. 3050	Dark turquoise
⁞ = Nr. 3094	Light blue	⁞ = Nr. 3040	Turquoise
⁞ = Nr. 3077	Blue	⁞ = Nr. 3139	Light turquoise

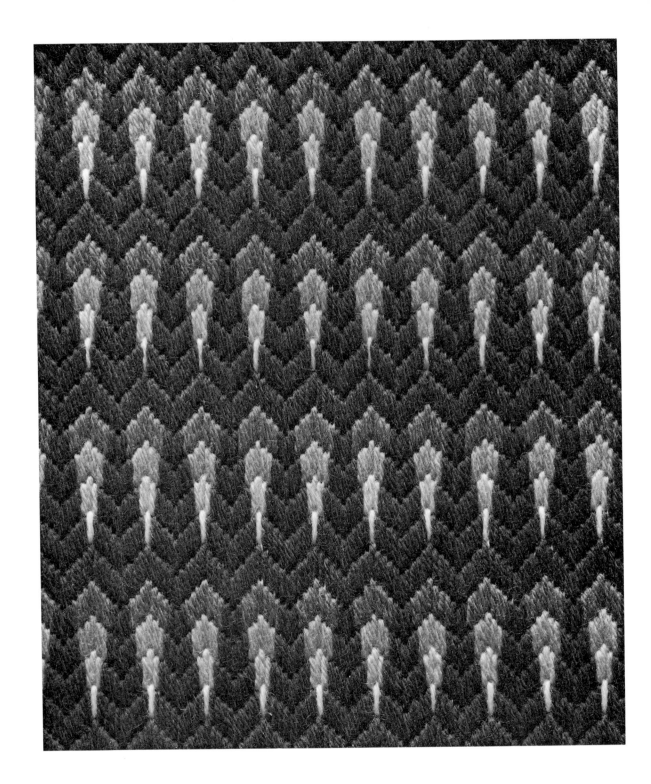

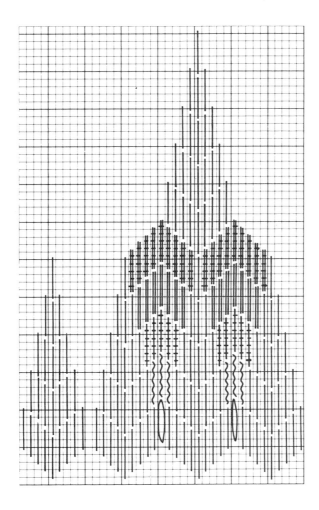

Instead of the single coloured red spire, you could use four to five graduated colour shades. This will make the pattern appear busier.

| = Nr. 3153   Red
◊ = Nr. 3222   White
≀ = Nr. 3445   Lightest blue
⋮ = Nr. 3094   Light blue
‖ = Nr. 3077   Mid blue
⋮ = Nr. 3030   Dark blue

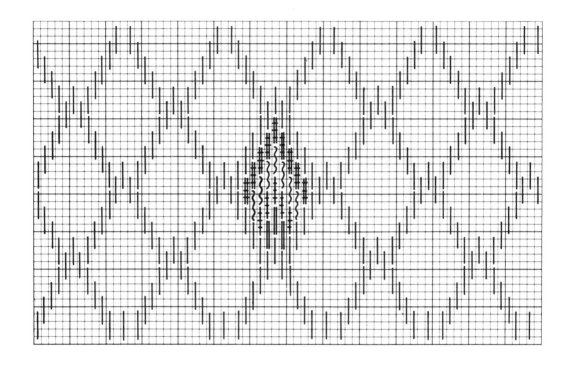

To begin with, embroider the dark turquoise
borders of the rhombuses only over a fairly large
area. It is easier to keep a check on your work
this way.

| = Nr. 3078   Dark turquoise
‖ = Nr. 3898   Red
⊧ = Nr. 3222   White
≀ = Nr. 3139   Light turquoise
‡ = Nr. 3140   Mid turquoise

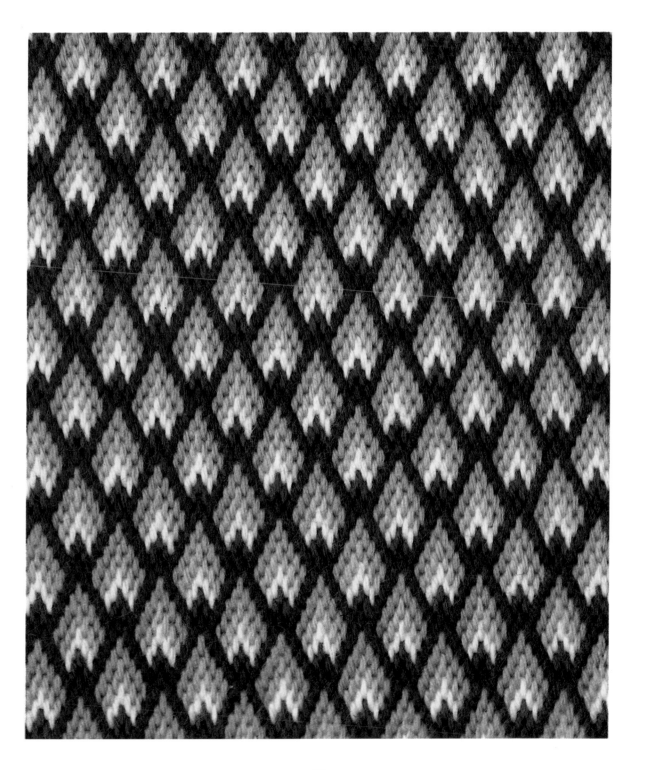

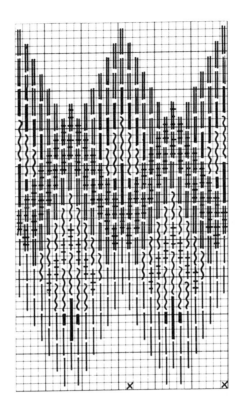

This pattern looks simple but you can easily
make a mistake in counting. So take extra
care when working it.

	= Nr. 3898	Red
	= Nr. 3056	Black
	= Nr. 3015	Dark yellow
	= Nr. 3229	Pale yellow
|| = Nr. 3054	Dark blue
	= Nr. 3145	Light blue

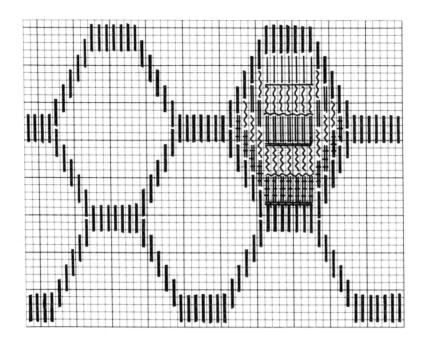

Start by embroidering a fairly large section of the black
borders, then fill in the rhombuses, red or green
alternately. A horizontal stitch is worked over threads in
the same colour as indicated.

| = Nr. 3056   Black
| = Nr. 3290   Lightest red
  = Nr. 3085   Lightest green

} = Nr. 3893   Light red
  = Nr. 3087   Light green

‖ = Nr. 3895   Mid red
  = Nr. 3043   Mid green

} = Nr. 3896   Dark red
  = Nr. 3044   Dark green

‡ = Nr. 3898   Darkest red
  = Nr. 3089   Darkest green

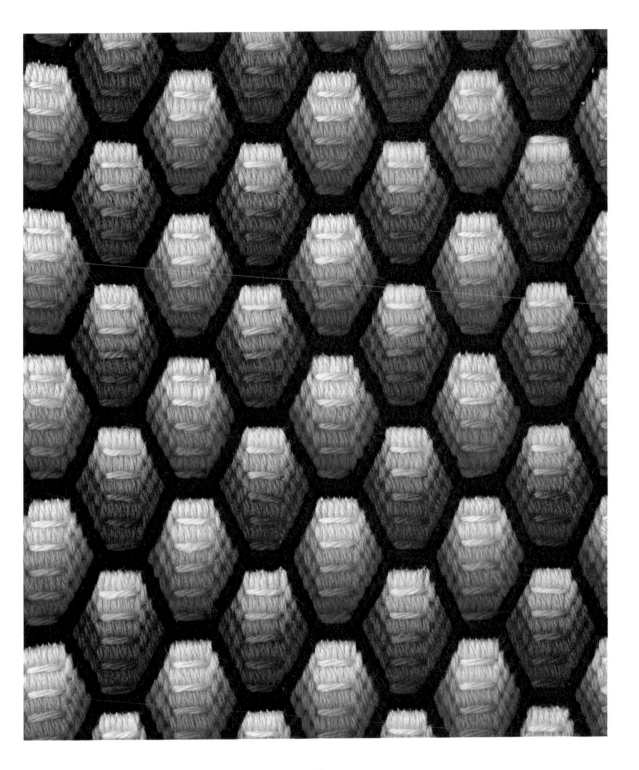

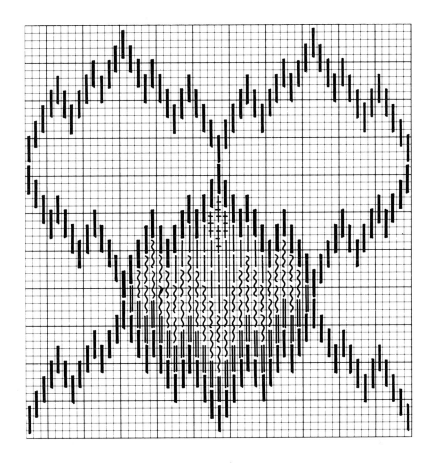

Embroider a fairly large area of the brown borders first, then fill these colours in in turn.

| = Nr. 3137   Brown
‖ = Nr. 3158   Dark lilac
≀ = Nr. 3157   Mid lilac
| = Nr. 3155   Pale lilac
‡ = Nr. 3204   White

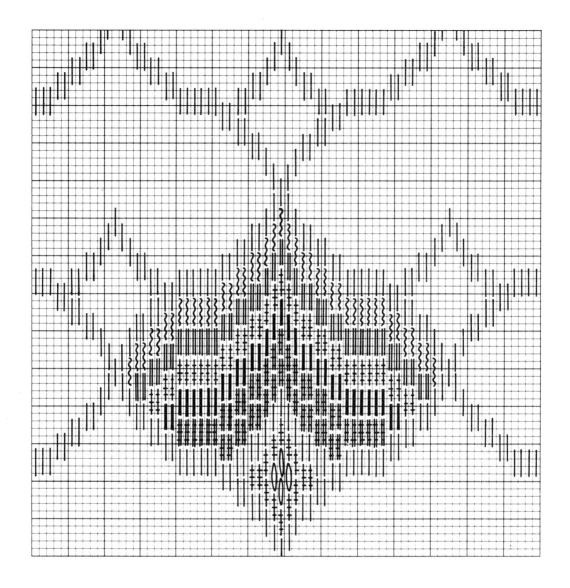

Embroider a fairly large area of the white borders, then fill these
in colour by colour.

| = Nr. 3222 White | = Nr. 3139 Lightest turquoise
} = Nr. 3078 Dark turquoise   ‖ = Nr. 3445 Grey
‖ = Nr. 3050 Turquoise   ◊ = Nr. 3896 Red
‡ = Nr. 3140 Light turquoise

74

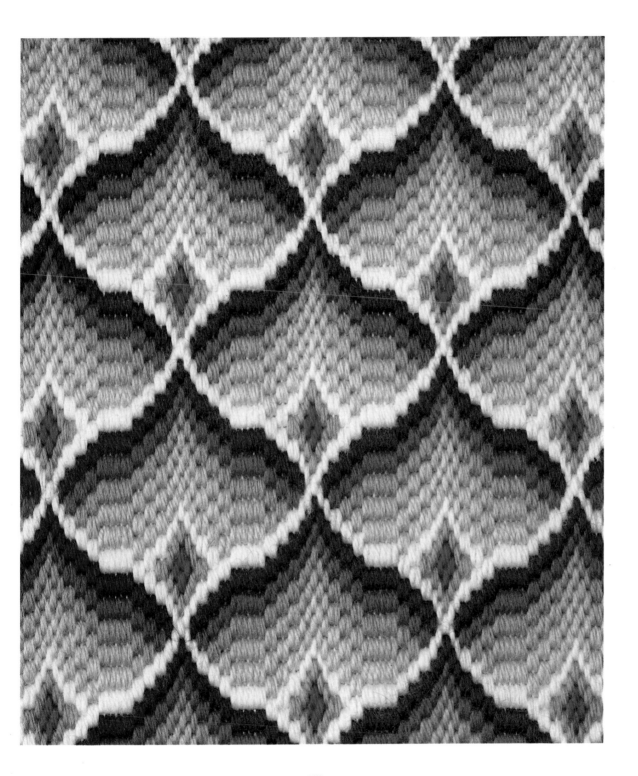

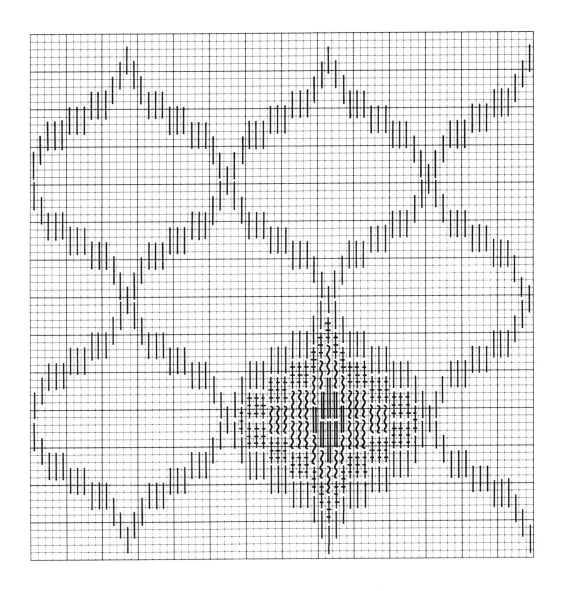

| = Nr. 3078   Dark green
‡ = Nr. 3158   Lilac
{ = Nr. 3155   Light lilac
‖ = Nr. 3140   Turquoise

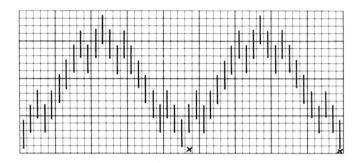

For larger areas it is more advantageous to
embroider the pattern over 6 threads (stepping up
or down 3 threads).

Dark brown	Nr. 3136
Mid brown	Nr. 3065
Light brown	Nr. 3134
Dark green	Nr. 3180
Mid green	Nr. 3177
Light green	Nr. 3175
Dark red	Nr. 3898
Mid red	Nr. 3896
Light red	Nr. 3895
Dark blue	Nr. 3058
Mid blue	Nr. 3146
Light blue	Nr. 3144

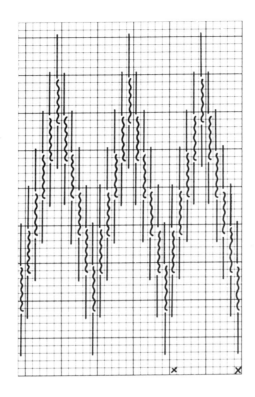

Embroider over 6 threads and then
step up or down by 5 threads.

Dark blue	Nr. 3034
Mid blue	Nr. 3058
Light blue	Nr. 3146
Lightest blue	Nr. 3144
White	Nr. 3222
Light green	Nr. 3173
Mid green	Nr. 3175
Dark green	Nr. 3177

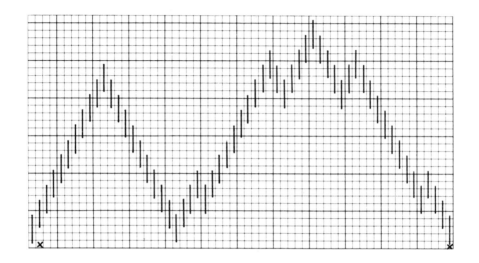

For larger surfaces you can also work
this pattern over 6 threads. The points
will then be very steep.

White	Nr. 3204
Light blue	Nr. 3094
Mid blue	Nr. 3077
Dark blue	Nr. 3030
Lilac	Nr. 3157
Dark blue	Nr. 3030
Mid blue	Nr. 3077
Light blue	Nr. 3094

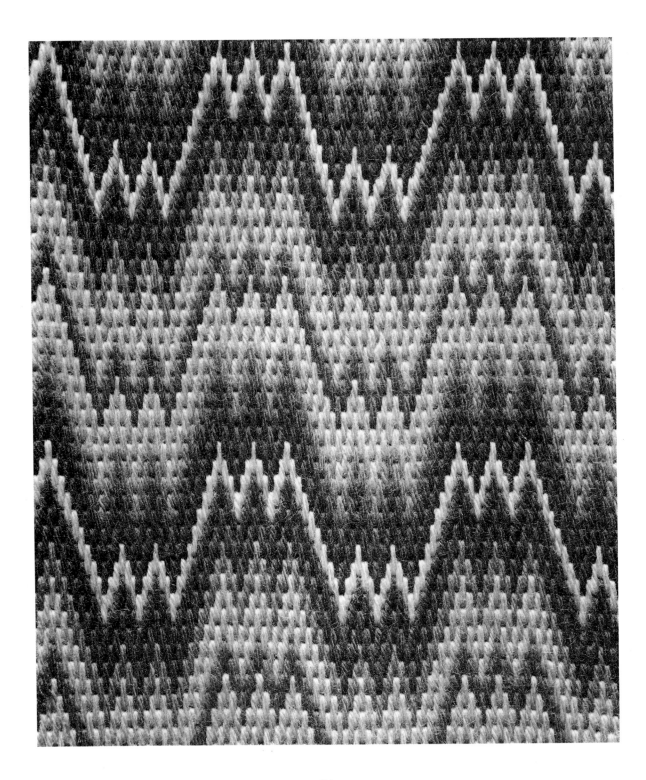

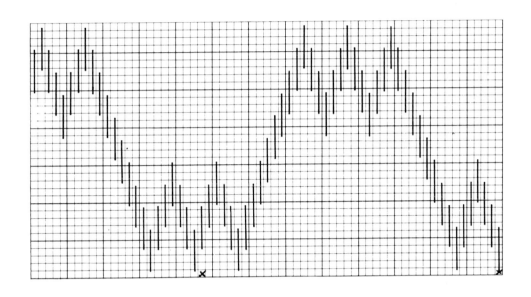

Darkest green	Nr. 3180
Dark green	Nr. 3177
Mid green	Nr. 3175
Light green (twice)	Nr. 3173
Red	Nr. 3896
Light green (twice)	Nr. 3173
Mid green	Nr. 3175
Dark green	Nr. 3177
Darkest green	Nr. 3180
Pink	Nr. 3290

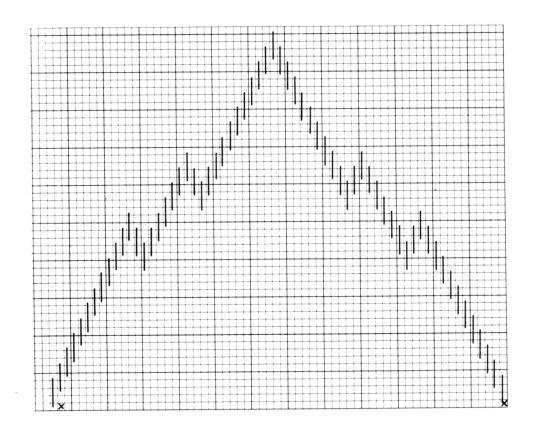

This pattern can also be embroidered over 6
threads and stepped up or down by 3 threads.

Red	Nr. 3011
Dark green	Nr. 3044
Mid green	Nr. 3043
Light green	Nr. 3087
White	Nr. 3204
Brown	Nr. 3040
White	Nr. 3204
Light green	Nr. 3087
Mid green	Nr. 3043
Dark green	Nr. 3044

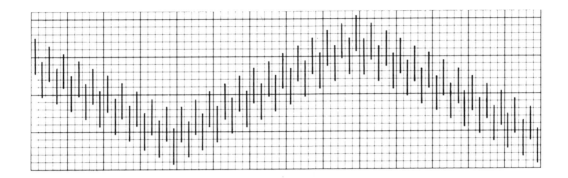

This pattern almost looks like
Tunisian crochet work where the
individual rows of colour interlock
like cog wheels.

Darkest yellow	Nr. 3016
Dark yellow	Nr. 3015
Mid yellow	Nr. 3013
Pale yellow	Nr. 3239
Mid yellow	Nr. 3013
Dark yellow	Nr. 3015
Darkest yellow	Nr. 3016

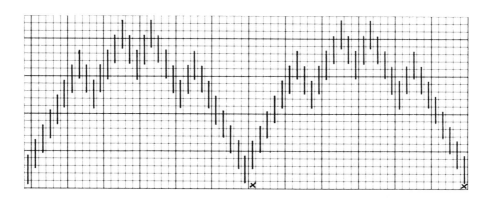

Darkest green	Nr. 3089
Dark green	Nr. 3044
Mid green	Nr. 3043
Light green	Nr. 3087
Lightest green	Nr. 3085

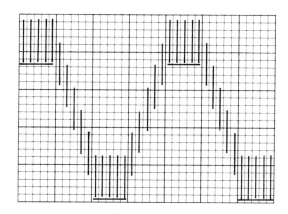

Embroider over 6 threads and at times step
up or down by 3 threads. Embroider
horizontally over the 5 threads lying next to
one another with the same colour.

Darkest brown	Nr. 3137
Dark brown	Nr. 3136
Mid brown	Nr. 3065
Light brown (twice)	Nr. 3134

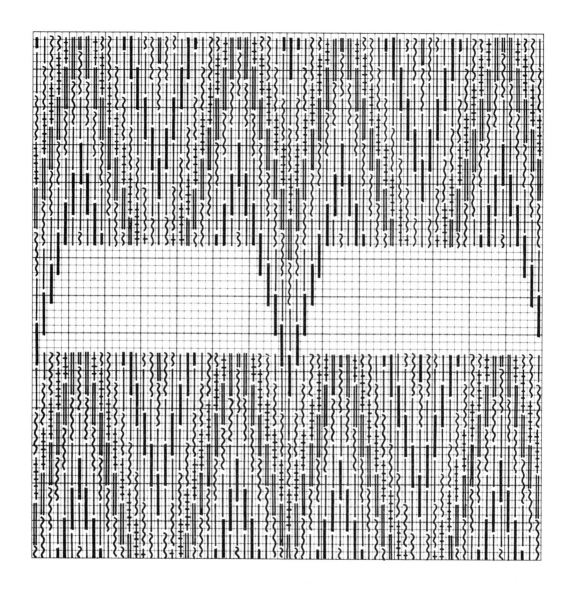

Embroider the points first, then insert the bands into the
vacant spaces (see the small diagram).

| = Nr. 3040   Brown
| = Nr. 3085   Lightest green
} = Nr. 3087   Light green   *Small diagram, right:*
| = Nr. 3043   Mid green | = Nr. 3895   Light red
‡ = Nr. 3044   Dark green   } = Nr. 3896   Mid red
                                       ‖ = Nr. 3898   Dark red

Of further interest . . .

Traditional Samplers

*The world's most beautiful samplers
for you to make at home*

Regina Forstner

Here is the chance to make your own heirlooms!

The author explains the origins of samplers and how, over the long history of their production, the motifs and colours have evolved so that your creations will have the genuine traditional look of your grandmother's and great grandmother's.

Collected together in this book are some of the most beautiful motifs and patterns gathered from original samplers all over the world. The colours used are as close as possible to the original colours in these very special examples of the art of the sampler.

Advice is given by the author on choice of materials — needles, yarn, fabric and so on — and easy-to-follow charts make creating your own traditional sampler easier than ever before.